The Voices of the Queens

The harrowing stories of Henry VIII's six wives told through poetry

Tessy Braun

The Voice of Six Tudor Queens

The Voice of Six Tudor Queens

Copyright © 2019 Tessy Braun

No part of this book may be used or reproduced in any manner without written permission from the author except for the use of brief quotations in a book review.

All rights reserved.

ISBN:
978-1-70107-5023

The Voice of Six Tudor Queens

The Voice of Six Tudor Queens

Preface

For many years I have enjoyed a fascination with the Tudor dynasty. I have been lucky to visit many historic sites including Hampton Court Palace and the Tower of London, as well as the less well known Tudor Sites across the country such as Acton Court and Newark Park near Bristol UK.

This small book comprises of a poem for each of Henry VIII's six wives. Their stories are told from their own voices, and are historically accurate. I really hope that you enjoy them.

Additionally there are two poems inside about the King's pleasure palace, Hampton Court Palace in East Molesey, London, and Acton Court, where Henry stayed with Anne Boleyn on his tour of South West of England in 1535.

The Voice of Six Tudor Queens

The Voice of Six Tudor Queens

Contents

Acknowledgements

Catherine of Aragon	**1**
Anne Boleyn	**5**
Jane Seymour	**9**
Anne of Cleves	**11**
Catherine Howard	**13**
Catherine Parr	**17**
Hampton Court Palace	**21**
Acton Court	**25**

About the Author - 29

The Voice of Six Tudor Queens

The Voice of Six Tudor Queens

Acknowledgements

Thank you to those who always encourage my writing, in particular Billy Harrington (**@thepoetbillyharrington** on Instagram).

My lovely mum, Rosemary, is also a source of inspiration, particularly when it comes to my Tudor poetry as she too harbours a keen interest in this captivating period.

In addition, of course, please take the time to think of the six queens who lived in the 16th century and what arduous hardships befell them.

The Voice of Six Tudor Queens

The Voice of Six Tudor Queens

Catherine of Aragon

A Princess leaving my Spanish realm,
I Catherine, with my captain at the helm,
longing to see mamá y papá again,
fearing of life, no longer the same.

Betrothed since the age of three,
I sailed across the ocean to thee,
to Arthur, my English Prince and heir,
to the throne, of which I soon would share.

I was just sixteen years of age,
sailing into a life pre-arranged,
not imagining how fate would rule
(my reign to end in a way so cruel).

We were married in fifteen hundred and one,
tragically our marriage had but begun,
when we were parted from one another,
and then I was to marry Henry, your brother.

How cruel and unforgiving life was to me,
I, true Queen of England so withdrawn,
how could I forgive him for what *he* did?
(My crime was that no son did live).

Mary sweet Mary, child of mine,
no longer in the Monarch's line.
He, the King, denied me her touch,
I missed my sweet Mary, so very much.

I'm dying now - life has almost left,
fifty years and now with poisoned flesh.
My faithful maid flocks to my side,
and in my last days to him I write -

"**M**y most dear lord, husband and king,
I pardon you for everything.
I pray that God will pardon you too,
please give to my maids what they are due,

The Voice of Six Tudor Queens

I commend unto you, Mary our daughter,
beseeching you to be a good father,
mine eyes desire you above all things,
from your only true wife,
Catherine the Queen".

The Voice of Six Tudor Queens

Anne Boleyn

You were my good Lord
and handsome you once were,
though your affection over me
had caused quite some stir.
For England adored Catherine,
who was your Queen before,
and they had the *audacity* to call me
a "Goggle eyed whore!".

Your love first fell on my sister
in the French Court,
but your lust for her,
like many girls
was really rather short.
My seductive dark brown eyes
captured your kindly attention,
yet to become a mere mistress,
was never my chosen intention.

The Voice of Six Tudor Queens

It wasn't long before you understood
it was *"Queen or nothing"*,
with your dreams of son and heir,
this only inspired your lusting.
Wolsey got to work
with the Pope to arrange the divorce,
he gave you false hope that it would be
just a matter of course.

You clung to the view
marriage to *her* was against God's Law,
for she had lain in bed
with your dear brother before.
Yet Pope Clement VII
would not fight our cause,
so you broke from the Catholic Church
and its ridiculous rules.

For me! My goodly Lord,
for me you changed the Christian faith!
(How could anyone have known
I'd soon be fallen from your grace?)
but then, instead of a goodly prince,
I bore you a female child,
and with the loss of others,

The Voice of Six Tudor Queens

it seems God would have you riled.

I was never very popular
and many thought me cursed,
rumours spread I had six fingers,
warts and that is not the worst.
I couldn't give the King a son,
so my cruel demise began,
they made it up - I didn't lie with my brother,
or take another man.

Fallen from your favour
and your attention now on Jane,
my father's greedy ambition
had put us all in shame.
They made it all up,
Smeaton my dear friend,
they tortured him until
he said what they *wanted* to hear.
(Yet he met his death on Tower Hill).

My goodly lord I spent nights and days preparing for
my leave of this world,
My brother gone, my heart did grieve.

It's agonisingly postponed
for the swordsman's arrival, yet
he travels so kindly from France
to slice through my little neck.

"**A**nd thus I take my leave
of the world and of you all,
oh Lord have mercy on me,
to God I commend my soul".
and with my ladies sobbing
silently by my side,
my head falls to the ground
but my soul is still alive!

Jane Seymour

Loved was I, cherished quite,
for I brought him a steady light,
I was not wicked, fierce or strong,
in his kingly eyes I did no wrong.

As Anne's lady in waiting, I could see
the King's attention fall on me,
just a day after she lost her head
the king promised to wed me instead.

We married yet I was never crowned,
for that pesky plague was still around.
I was kind and compassionate to Mary,
All of court thought me pleasant and caring.

Soon I was with child - my belly swelled,
not foreseeing the sorrow, the future held.
After a labour of two nights and three days,
I was fiercely struck with agonising pain.

The Voice of Six Tudor Queens

I died! Leaving my son with no mother.
He mourned, he could not love another.
Yet there was good news
throughout the court,
for the King had the son
he had long sought!

He always *thought* I was his favourite wife,
but I wonder if I hadn't lost my life,
perhaps he would have tired soon after,
it's likely my life would have been a disaster.

Now we lie together once more,
at Windsor Castle in
'The Chapel of St George'.
Edward ruled at the tender age of nine,
but tuberculosis took him,
poor child of mine.

Anne of Cleves

I was the plain German Princess,
Holbein came to paint my face,
so that my presence Henry could witness,
a fine portrait for his grace.

Cromwell did quite insist
that a match was made with us.
In the wake of the "Truce of Nice"
it would not be a marriage unjust.

One might say that I was the lucky one,
for I came out of it all unscathed,
for Henry did not find me pretty,
I was not the woman he craved.

He said I was ugly and *most* unclean,
yet he was the one with the odour.
His ulcer repulsively obscene,
and he thought me mediocre!?

When an annulment he asked of me,
I'd have been a fool to object,
so I agreed to it wholeheartedly,
this would *surely* save my neck?

The "King's dear sister" I was known,
he gave me Richmond Palace and more.
I was quite happy to give up the throne,
his generosity could not be ignored.

I, the only wife in Westminster Abbey,
some have found my tomb hard to find,
I was aged only forty-one when I passed,
and I was the last of his wives to die.

The Voice of Six Tudor Queens

Catherine Howard

I was but a child, not grown in years or mind.
life was cut short
and I left this cruel world behind.

On the 13th February
on death's path I tread,
when Henry VIII cuts off my sweet head!

My demise, though tragic,
was not foreseen,
despite the fate of the last fallen queen,
my first cousin Anne Boleyn…

*(I had briefly forgot,
that she had laid her head upon the block!).*

Yet fancy of court and royal life
was too appetizing,
with my flirtatious and fun loving nature,
was it surprising

that the ever growing wider Henry VIII
became so besotted
with my pretty young face?

I was his rose without a thorn,
but I found him disgusting.
His hideous ulcer repulsed me
and with his gut busting,
is it any wonder I looked about the Court
for something better,
of course I had my eyes set
on Thomas Culpeper!

I was immature, and raised
in a house of permissiveness.
My greatest crime
was my emotional silliness.
They came to take me
"give me mercy" I screamed,
for some hope still remained
that I might be redeemed.

The Voice of Six Tudor Queens

Yet down the river I went
to the Tower by water,
passing under London Bridge
I am reminded of the slaughter
that awaits me.
I am asked to prepare my soul for death,
I ask for the block,
to see how I will place myself best.

I could barely speak, yet confessed
my wrong doing in a weak voice.
I knelt, and with one quick swing of the axe my meek
life was gone,
my body covered with a cloak
and taken away
by my ladies,
to the Chapel of St Peter in chains.

The Voice of Six Tudor Queens

Catherine Parr

Last, but by no means least,
I wed Henry VIII, hideous and obese,
at Hampton Court Palace,
we made our vows
to be man and wife as law allows.

It was fifteen forty-three,
you had grown quite smitten with me,
you were a king
who could not be refused,
so this was the life that I *had* to choose.

With plague around the London streets,
for six months we stayed away
in our palace retreat,
in company together we built a foundation,
and we got along well, without hesitation.

The Voice of Six Tudor Queens

It helped that we had interests shared
of music, archery and hunting we both cared,
when you fought in France
for the very last time,
you left me to reign
as if the throne were mine.

I loved Mary and Elizabeth as my own,
and watched over them
until they were grown,
restoring your daughters
to the succession line,
and I cared for Edward
(but that poor lamb died).

Some say I couldn't have possibly
loved you truly, dear,
being a tyrant and filling your
kingdom with fear,
but I accepted this life as God's true will,
(and made quite sure
you had *no* reason to kill),

The Voice of Six Tudor Queens

but when you took a last breath
into your lungs
I was relieved for my life had just begun,
now free to re-marry,
with riches, I could rejoice,
and Thomas Seymour was my choice!

So now with my true love
I was reconciled,
A miracle happened
when I became with child,
but with my wildest dreams,
came my death curse,
I left my sweet daughter
eight days after her birth.

I was laid to rest at St Mary's Chapel,
in my beautiful home at Sudeley Castle,
but after more than two hundred years,
my coffin was found
and my flesh re-appeared!

Wrapped up snuggly in cloth,
resting in peace,
disturbed from my slumber,
ripped open my sheets,
the flesh on my arm
was still moist and white,
and when they unearthed
me I gave them a fright!

After my embalmed wax linen
was cut and frayed,
my skin turned brown
and my flesh decayed,
but taken from me was a lock of hair,
and a tooth of mine for all to share.

Hampton Court Palace

We start at Base Court,
a fine and impressive entry -
imagine courtiers bustling
back and forth, in the 16th century.
The awe hits me fiercely
like a deep rooted intimacy,
this palace of red brick
is a wonderment of history.

Henry VIII's kitchens -
enormous and beyond belief,
roasting up wild boar,
deer, oxen and beef.
The cooks sweltering
with exhaustion and working tirelessly,
to feed the four hundred mouths
of the palace's entirety.

The Voice of Six Tudor Queens

Standing in the Great Hall
at Hampton Court Palace,
breathing in energy
five centuries long since passed.
The presence of Anne Boleyn
and each ill-fated queen,
echoing wall to wall
where celebrations were once seen.

Tapestries then shimmering
and sparkling with gold,
absorbed all the whispering
and stories once told,
I close my eyes to come close
to the spirits and ghosts,
where once king and queens
had liked to dance the most.

The Voice of Six Tudor Queens

Through the Great Watching Chamber
to the gallery, where
Catherine escaped her guards
and ran to reach Henry at prayer,
to the Chapel Royal - she screamed
for mercy in attempt to spare
her young sweet life, but to no avail,
for the King had *no* care.

The Royal Pew -
stand where he would have once prayed,
the view of the chapel where
Jane Seymour's heart stayed,
with its intricate ceiling
of blue and gold sure to amaze -
a church where for centuries
Monarchs have praised.

Hampton Court Palace
is a mix of bygone times,
yet my affection always wanders
to the first two wives
and the gruesome way Anne
and the fifth lost their lives.
She wept, "Good Christian people,
I have come here to die".

Acton Court

Five hundred years ago,
a mere handshake away,
Henry VIII and his queen
had a visit to pay,
they spent two nights
at Acton Court,
during their mission
to gain more support.

Nearly black elm-wood
under my feet,
the exact same flooring
where king's soles once did meet.
What have the walls
in this chamber absorbed?
They must hold the secrets
and whispers once forged.

The Voice of Six Tudor Queens

Extravagant beauty
King Henry admired
and his tapestries hung here
just how he desired.
To imagine deeply
what happened in this home
sends shivers tingling
through my bones!

Oh Anne Boleyn,
Anne Boleyn,
if only you knew
the future, where in,
just nine months later
you'd be labelled a traitor,
and on May the 19th at 8 o'clock,
you'd lay your head down on the block…

The Voice of Six Tudor Queens

Now rescued from
a sorry state of disrepair,
no longer so shabby with no one to care.
Acton Court is restored
to its righteous glory,
and is awaiting to tell you
the rest of its story

The Voice of Six Tudor Queens

About the Author

Tessy has been writing poems and short stories since she was a child. Tucked away in her home you'll find boxes of diaries and journals that are testimony to her love of writing.

In addition to writing, Tessy is also a keen musician and enjoys playing the cello and violin. Tessy is a mother of two young boys and enjoys exploring the outdoors with them.

Tessy would be so grateful if you would like to leave a review of 'The Voice of Six Tudor Queens' on Amazon.

The Voice of Six Tudor Queens

Other titles from the author

For None Would Hear
A poetic story exploring the tragic consequences of domestic abuse.

Open Book
A collection of poetry exploring a range of themes including love, heartbreak, abuse, depression, parenting and loss.

The Midnight Masquerade
An enchanting poetic story celebrating community and love.

Travels with Tessy
A poetic journey throughout South West England and beyond.

In the Little Woodland Clearing
A narrative poem about child-eating faeries and the quest to restore peace in the little woodland clearing.

The Voice of Six Tudor Queens

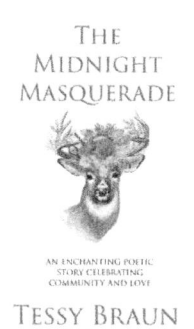

Printed in Great Britain
by Amazon